Doctor Music

Marianna Lima
Doctor Music

Published by BooxAi

ISBN: 978-965-578-147-2

Doctor Music

Marianna Lima

Music

WHAT IS MUSIC?

Music is a kind of art where the totality of musical sounds come together to form an artistic image. The main elements of music are: rhythm, meter, tempo, timbre, melody, harmony, polyphony, and instrumentation.

I would now like to touch upon each of them very briefly.

MODE

The mode is an important aesthetic part of music. It is a system of pitch connections that connect with the center sound. It is embodied in the scale in the sound system.

RHYTHM

Rhythm is the change of elements (sound, speech) in a specific period of time, which occurs in a certain sequence, frequency, and speed. And specifically in music, temporal organization through musical sounds.

Metre

Metre is a system of alternation of strong and weak rhythmic beats. It can be simple, complex, mixed, or variable. Each group that begins with the strongest beat makes up a beat.

Metronome

A metronome is a device that beats short periods with uniform beats. It is primarily used by musicians as an accurate tempo guide. It helps to develop a sense of rhythm and dynamics of performance.

Dynamics

Dynamics is the change of different forces, height, and change of that force.

Timbre

Timbre is the coloring of the sound that makes it possible to distinguish between the pitch sounds of different instruments. They are as diverse in both instruments and vocalists as you can guess.

Melody

Melody (translated from Greek: melodia - singing) is a musical thought expressed in unison, it is the main element of music.

A melody is a series of sounds organized by mode-intonation, rhythmic form, and certain structure.

Harmony

Harmony is a means of musical expression based on the combination of tones and the conjunction of consonants in their sequential movement. The basic sound form is the chord. The harmony is built according to a special mode pattern. The elements of harmony are cadence and modulation.

POLYPHONY

Polyphony is based on the simultaneous combination of two or more independent melodies.

INSTRUMENTATION

Instrumentation is a form of musical performance in the form of a chamber ensemble, orchestra, and other scores.

I hope you have got a general idea of the classical musical formulas. It's not the point, and it's not what we're here for. But knowing the rationale behind everything by looking at it from the point of view of the rules sometimes may be helpful... and sometimes it may disturb... I have higher education in music, I graduated from the conservatory, but the power, splendor, magic, and healing power of music is far beyond all kinds of rules, educational institutions as well as diplomas. By the way, I have more than twenty international diplomas from all over the world.

People always asked how I came back winning in all competitions. And it was always very difficult for me to explain what kind of power comes over me when I go on stage...And what magical energy I get from the universe... inexplicable... when I want to bring my music to people... It's not even me, but the music itself that controls me, and maybe one day earlier or later, I strongly believe that we just will be able to reach a level of consciousness, even higher than this, that through music we will be able to find alternative solutions for the treatment of seemingly complex diseases. It may be the most important discovery, or one of the discoveries, of the 21st century.

People will be able to achieve a level of self-management and self-healing where they will not need pills in most cases... That time is right now, which is why I'm writing this book, which I hope will help us all understand the ultimate purpose of music, which the universe has gifted us with...

The effect of music on our brain

Millions of years ago, music helped our distant ancestors survive. During evolution, the sense of rhythm developed, vocal tact became more complex, and vocal communication split between speech and music, which is older than Homo Sapiens appeared in Africa 200,000 years ago. Since then, music has become a very important part of humanity. It has a very strong effect on our brains. It activates instincts, causes conditioned reflexes, and associations that affect emotions help to overcome them and affect the pleasure center.

It happens in a very surprising way. Perhaps in the oldest art alone, we see the neurological effect of sound on the brain. It passes from the ear to the neurons of the brain, we can even unconsciously move with the rhythm and go from one state to another, changing our mood unconsciously. Therefore our actions, global quality of life, and even the most important steps depend on it. It is in our roots. It has a great impact in a radical sense - Swedish professor and psychologist Patrick Yuslin mentioned 7 reasons why music affects our emotions and behavior.

Even ancient Greek manuscripts say that "musical education is the most powerful weapon because rhythm and harmony penetrate the depths of the human soul. You can get rid of depression, anxiety, and neurological problems through music. Rhythm and harmony permeate the depths of the human soul. The music we listen to can feed our brains with a specific energy that creates a specific mood. And in fact, the children who attend the music school are calmer, adequate... But why...?

It is very interesting what quantum physicists found out... they discovered that the material world, which includes our human bodies, is vibrating on different levels. Music is a vibration, and it's no surprise that that vibration correlates with the vibration of our bodies.

The ancient physician Avicenna called music a non-medicinal method of healing along with diets, pills, and laughter. The Pythagoreans also noticed that music somehow affects a person interestingly. They used special tunes to deal with anger, then they had their math lessons with special music and found that the lessons were more active. In the 3rd century AD, the Parthuni kingdom built a special music center where people were cured of depression and mental anxiety. It is an interesting fact that, for example, in some countries, it is believed that the most healing sound is given by the bell, which can cure headaches and vein problems, and even helps to get rid of the evil eye and evil spirits.

The sound of the bell resonates with a clear ultrasonic resonant sound that can destroy viruses and neutralize dangerous diseases within seconds.

It is interesting which hemisphere of the brain we use to listen to music.

The areas of the brain that process the perception of music are generally located in about the same place in all of them: the right hemisphere in right-handed people and the left in left-handed people. And the left hemisphere is responsible for speech, that is, when producing music, the left hemisphere is also important. When singing a melody without words, the right hemisphere of the brain is used, but if the melody is accompanied by words, the left hemisphere is increasingly mobilized.

There is a new interesting fact. When a professional musician listens to music, there is a visible change in the right hemisphere for him and in the left hemisphere of a non-musician. People with musical education develop a greater strategy for organizing brain activity when listening to music, and the brain starts to work more actively. A study was done on the effects of disco music, which found that disco music has the same effect on some people as anti-depressant pills.

Therefore, we can control our mood and psychological state through music. For example, melodic, soft music causes a decrease in frequent EEG rhythms, while rhythmic music does the opposite.

Major music accelerates blood pressure, increases blood pressure, increases muscle pressure, and minor music, on the contrary, relaxes muscles and lowers blood pressure. March music promotes muscle activation, and some symphonic compositions can change the acidity of gastric juice. Different genres of music have a big impact even on our hormones and blood.

Some studies show that listening to music has the same effect that people get from taking drugs. For example, piano and violin relax the brain.

A study at the Institute of California showed that classical music lowers blood pressure. Another institute, in Budapest, concluded that classical music has a very good effect on sleep. They recruited 94 people aged 19-28 who had insomnia, and they listened to classical music every night for 3 weeks before going to sleep, and their sleep improved.

When a person listens to classical music, the center responsible for the art in the person's brain is activated, which can be seen on an MRI, and a harmonization occurs that boosts the person's immune system. It is interesting why so many teenagers prefer to listen to rock. The reason is that children are more rebellious at that age, and rock music inspires them and gives them the strength to express themselves.

I think it's already clear that music can affect us both positively and negatively.

But the most interesting and mysterious question remains whether we can heal people with music.

Music as a doctor

In 1991, Professor Yakov Levin developed a method by means which music cures insomnia, depression, and chronic stress when people listen to it at the expense of receiving their electroencephalogram. He called this method "Brain Music". It is done as follows. Electrodes are placed on the person's head, and the EEG is recorded for 5 minutes. The person is in a relaxed state with closed eyes, and the appropriate music is played. When the brain recognizes its sounds, its functional state improves, the functional state of the hemispheres improves, melatonin is activated, and a natural antioxidant, the sleep hormone, is produced.

In some countries, special CDs are sold, the names of which can be, for example, "Stomach", "Lungs", and "Liver", where there are compositions for treating these organs. I think most of us would prefer to be treated with this method rather than taking heavy pills with multiple side effects. That is why music therapy is becoming more and more popular and in demand. Pythagoras had clear group vocal performances in his music lessons where he noted that by creating harmony in music, we alone create harmony in our souls. A funny incident happened to him when once the great philosopher saw how a man wanted to set his girlfriend's house on fire because of jealousy. At that moment, a musician was standing on the street playing the flute. He asked the musician to play some quiet tunes. When the musician started playing quiet music, that jealous man changed his mood and changed his mind about burning down his girlfriend's house. And so Pythagoras was the first to compile a book of musical healing recipes where every disease had its melody.

In the middle ages, music therapy fell out of fashion, but in 1621 the English intellectual Robert Burton published the book "Anatomy of Melancholy", in which he explained how music could cure many nervous problems. In the 19th century, many European psychologists treated their visitors through music. It became more popular in the 20th century.

Mozart's music is most popular for having a healing effect. African music is also a very good influence. And hard rock and hip-hop are considered ineffective by doctors. Some musical instruments have a very strong effect on our brains; it's even, as I said, studied by doctors.

Music can clean the environment of negative energy, heal our bodies, and harmonize the energetic field.

For example, in ancient China, there was an intellectual named Sima Qian, who said that "music and melody shake our internal organs, affect our blood, penetrate the depths of our souls, and harmonize our true feelings. As you can already see in ancient Greece and China, even in ancient times already, some intelligent individuals realized this truth and even tried to heal people. It can already be considered objective and considered a scientific fact somewhere. However, the paradox is that from a scientific point of view there is no such thing as mental energy, or any immeasurable, very important effect of any energy affecting the physical body. And here it becomes clear that there is... yes, it exists as well as the physical... Actually, we can say that a physiological reaction to specific music exists, and it has been proven.

Our organism itself is rhythmic. Our heart works in rhythms, we breathe in rhythms. Music makes us squirm, we can feel it on our skin immediately, and it controls our mood on a subconscious and even unconscious level over time. In some countries, "Harp Therapy" using the Harp is very popular, and if doctors have reached the level of consciousness that they practice these methods specifically for patients, imagine that if you understand the magical power of music, you won't even need pills...

Today, the harp itself is mainly used as an instrument with a healing vibration... but I think science still has a lot to discover, also about other musical instruments. I am going to study how each instrument affects the human brain and body and apply these tools in my album, dedicated to this topic.

Effects of music on various diseases

Stroke - an interesting study was done in Germany in 2016. Neuroscientists conducted it at the Hannover Institute of Physiology. They asked patients with extensive stroke and minimal mobility to create sounds in a three-dimensional field on a wooden box, with each hand movement producing a sound of varying intensity. These people first played a few sounds, then amazingly began to remember them, create their melody and play it.

The primary goal of this experiment was to create a sound that a person wants to hear and to activate motor skills through coordinated movements. The experiment was successful. Among the positive results were the reduction of pain in joints and damaged limbs, improvement of the patient's memory, and improvement of their emotional state.

The rehabilitation of people who have had a stroke is a very important task that doctors all over the world are dealing with. Physical therapy is not the end for complete rehabilitation, and here music therapy can play a very decisive and important role.

Epilepsy - People who have epilepsy have a spot in the brain area that gets excited from time to time, and the funny thing is that it's in the same area that our brain perceives and processes music. Interestingly, people with epilepsy and people without epilepsy perceive music very differently. People with epilepsy have synchronization of brain activity with the sounds of music, which results in reduced epileptic activity. Experience shows that regularly listening to Mozart's melodies can reduce the frequency of seizures. Here is another scientific proof of how music can be the best doctor.

Parkinson's disease - recently, doctors in London announced that singing helps people with Parkinson's by having a good effect on them. Singing helps to develop the speech apparatus and to some extent reduces the manifestations of the disease. Music therapy is very effective in treating Parkinson's. Drumming also has a good effect.

Alzheimer's disease - Doctors have discovered that music also has a very good effect on people with Alzheimer's. It increases the appetite and helps to correct the psychological state. People with Alzheimer's are advised to listen to children's songs, dance songs, and sing karaoke. All this contributes to mental and motor activity. And lullabies can help ease them to sleep. The doctors note that at a certain stage of the disease, it is difficult for them to express their emotions, and in those cases, their relatives can choose music as a mediator of communication.

Music in psychotherapy

This is certainly the most extensive area of application of music in medicine. Music therapy is used today as a powerful method of combating stress, fear, depression, and anxiety. It helps in the fight against mental disorders and neuroses.

If people with such diseases play musical instruments themselves, they can get rid of their disturbing emotions. It is an interesting fact that in women, the activity of the prefrontal cortex responsible for emotions is activated, while in men, it decreases.

Amyotrophic lateral sclerosis - people who have this disease, together with rehabilitation procedures, perform music therapy three times a week, which has an effective influence. The result is visible after a month.

Cardiovascular diseases - Reducing anxiety and preventing stress is very important for people with heart disease. In that case, individual music therapy is performed, after which blood pressure is checked. It affects a person in the same way as pills.

Bronchial asthma - As we know, all diseases that are related to our immune system are also directly related to our psychological state.

In particular, bronchial asthma is helped by practicing vocal music, which helps to activate the lower diaphragm.

The doctors performed a test that showed that after one hour of music therapy, the picture of people's blood parameters changed. Leukocytes and neutrophils increased five times, lymphocytes- four times. After that test, doctors use music therapy for this kind of disease as well.

Music as an anti-aging medicine

Doctors have also begun to use it in neurohormonal correction with hearing aids. It's called mezzo-forte therapy. This method affects the human hormonal system, contributing to tissue regeneration as well as psychology.

Here, a magnetic mask is used, which is placed on the visitor's face. It emits acoustic signals. Headphones are also used. In other parts of the body that are biologically active, acoustic reflectors are worn. All this action causes a specific hormonal reaction, and at the same time, these signals affect the skin. Blood circulation improves, and the psychological state of a person also improves. I will address this topic in another book because I have always thought that rejuvenation projects or programs are one of the priorities these days.

Oncology, cancer - Research has been done for cancer patients. They listened to pop, rock, classical, and spiritual music. Spiritual music was found to have the strongest effect. Through music therapy, they can take fewer pills and also get rid of nervous anxiety. Today, doctors understand very well that music therapy can be a very powerful, important tool for cancer prevention. But diseases of this kind inspire fear, many believe that it is impossible to defeat it, and it is of great importance to defeat it. Why?... Every simplest action is first dictated by our brain, momentarily, after which the body, emotion, and physiology go into action. If, subconsciously, a person will think that he can never overcome any disease, no pills, no therapy, no best doctor in the world can ever help. Regardless of how good the pill, the therapy, and the professional are, the first and most important factor is the person's attitude toward the problem. Psychologists today have come to that conclusion indirectly after doing a lot of research. When a person knows that a given pill will help him get rid of pain, it will help more or less if a person knows that nothing will help him, nothing will help him.

If we make a smooth transition to psychology, we will understand a lot about ourselves. I think the most important thing for all of us is self-knowledge to understand who we are, what we want from this world, what we want to give, what we want to take, and what we want to leave after us...

Since this book is not about psychology, we will not delve into radical psychology, but to understand the effect of music therapy on the human brain, I think we should start from the roots.

Most importantly, regardless of any therapy, treatment method, or pill, it doesn't matter what we always have to realize that you deserve to be treated, and that's exactly how it will be, regardless of extraneous circumstances, other people's opinions, situations...

Facts about the effect of music on our brain

Today we know about 17 musical genres, which in turn are divided into sub genres, and despite this variety, everyone chooses his genre.

1. Can music make us happy?

American theorist Jerrold Levinson said that musical language is as important as our spoken language. Music contains a more powerful emotional reserve. When listening to music, we have two types of emotion: receptive and eliminative. In other words, a person can even experience emotion through music that he has never experienced in real life.

2. How background noise affects creativity?

It is an interesting fact that during high waves of noise, the human brain is overloaded and tries not to focus on distracting facts and circumstances, and the information that is primary for him becomes of better quality.

3. Is it possible to predict a person's character by knowing their musical taste?

For the first time, an investigation was conducted at HWU University, as a result of which it became clear that there is a direct connection between a person's personality and musical taste. This experiment involved 36,518 young people who had to listen to 104 different genres of music and categorize themselves. And in the 2nd round, everyone had a partner whose personality traits they had to guess based on their musical taste. They had 5 traits for this: 1 readiness for new experience, 2 extroversion, 3. politeness, 4. piety, 5. emotional balance.

And here, the experts came to this conclusion:

1. Blues listeners are creative, sociable, educated, and generous.
2. Jazz listeners- art lovers as well as arrogant.
3. Classical music lovers are more introverted and have high dignity.
4. People who love rap are more sociable and egotistical.
5. Opera fans are friendly and polite.
6. Country listeners are purposeful and get on well with people easily.
7. Reggae fans are arrogant, creative, and lazy.
8. Dance disco music fans are extravagant.
9. Indie-loving people have low self-esteem and are not well-educated.
10. People who listen to rock / also heavy metal/ have low self-esteem, but have the potential to advance in great art.

These are the results based on the first experiment.

4. Is it worth listening to music while driving?

An experiment was conducted at Ben Gurion University in Israel, which proved that music while driving has a positive effect on a person. It was found that drivers make more mistakes when they drive without music playing.

5. Is there any common connection between music and our intelligence?

As we already know, when a child is engaged in music from an early age, it has a good effect on later mental development. Also, scientists have come to the opinion that if a person engages in music for a longer time, it is a stimulus for the harmonious work of the right and left hemispheres.

6. Why is it harmful to talk on the phone too much?

There is a sign on the Tokyo subway that says talking on the phone disturbs other people. It also has a scientific explanation.

A study at the University of San Diego showed that a person's attention is more focused on a phone conversation when he is not listening to both parties than when he is listening to the entire dialogue.

82% of people find talking on the phone in public places annoying.

7. How does music affect training?

American expert Leonard Ayres discovered that cyclists make more flexible movements when riding a bicycle while listening to rhythmic music. Music masks fatigue signals.

When the body is physically tired, it sends a signal to the brain that the muscles need time to recover. But music counteracts that signal, harmonizing it and telling the brain to continue doing physical work.

In 2012, a study was conducted that showed that cyclists used 70% less oxygen while listening to music during exercise. Indeed, the athletes themselves did not feel it. But our organism is very smart, flexible, and feels and appreciates every useful thing...

Effects of music on animals

Scientists have found that animals perceive music in a different way, unlike humans, because they hear sounds more clearly and deeply than humans.

An experiment was conducted on animals, which showed that animals also have their preferred creations. They were the works of Beethoven, Bach, Mozart, and Schumann.

The dogs

In 2012, an experiment was conducted at the University of Colorado, which showed that 117 dogs who listened to classical music fell asleep, many just relaxed, and for example, metal music made them more aggressive.

Scientists have found that the larger the size of the dog, the closer its reaction to music is to that of a human.

The cats

Cats are very beautiful and mysterious animals. At the University of Lisbon, it was found that 12 cats that had to be sterilized listened to 3 different genres of music, and their reactions were better to classical music. Today, experts and doctors believe that soon music therapy will have a larger collaboration with painkillers.

Today, you can find music on the Internet specifically for cats. Younger and older cats respond more strongly to music than middle-aged cats.

The monkeys

American scientists found out that in the case of monkeys, music increases appetite and relaxation. They were very well influenced by Metallica's "Of wolf and man".

Monkeys are said to be similar to humans in some ways, but musically they are very different, as experience has shown.

The cows

It's very funny, but the reaction of cows to Beethoven's works is very good. Also, REM's music had a good influence on them. Scientists conducted an experiment lasting 9 weeks, using songs with fast and slow rhythms, followed by 12 hours of silence. The reaction of the cows to the melodic compositions was the best. When the cows listened to Beethoven's compositions, each gave 0.73 liters more milk per day.

The elephants

Elephants are not only very fond of music but are also very good musicians themselves. They are very fond of violin and wind instruments. Defender of nature Richard Leroy has adopted 16 elephants in Thailand and created the "Thailand Elephant Ensemble". They play accordion and steel drums.

But they don't like loud music. They don't like rock music.

The birds

Birds respond to music in the same way as humans. Experts at Emory University studied the birds' brains and found that when male birds heard a song, the sounds made by female birds were the same as the cardiac reaction. They also react like humans to sounds they don't like.

The fish

These amazing animals can even distinguish composers.

In 2013, the journal Behavioral Processes reported the results of a study suggesting that goldfish can listen to and distinguish compositions from compositions they have heard many times.

Keio University experts used pieces by Stravinsky and Bach, feeding the fish each time their melodies were played. After that experiment, when the same fish were given food without the given melodies but accompanied by another melody, they refused to eat the food. Yes, such amazing goldfish exist.

.

The effect of music on the water

Music changes water content. Many of us know Japanese scientist Emoto Masaru, who wrote a book in 1999 entitled "The Hidden Messages in Water". The book brought him worldwide fame. Several experiments are described in the book, where it is reflected that under the influence of music, the content of water, and the type of molecules, completely change. He placed a glass of plain water between the 2 pillars. Music echoed from the pillars. After that, the water was cooled, after which the molecules and atoms were studied under a microscope.

The result stunned the whole world. Many pure crystals have been created that follow certain rules. Every piece of music creates a different molecular form. For example, Tchaikovsky's Swan Lake created a shape resembling a bird's feather, and Mozart's Symphony No. 40 also created a very beautiful model. So did Vivaldi's Four Seasons. Scientists have also proven the opposite effect. In other words, by playing the wrong, ugly music, the water crystals got the wrong ugly shapes.

Maybe not everyone knows about water being so emotional, but don't forget that 70% of our body is water. And what does that

mean?... Music has a great influence on our body even from a physiological point of view.

Why does a water molecule change its shape?

The atomic analysis gave us the answer to this question. Masaru believed that the energy of water was called "hado", which means a certain wave of oscillation of electrons in the nucleus of an atom. According to Masaru, the energy of water was called "hado", which means a certain wave of oscillation of electrons in the nucleus of an atom.

A musical tone is an energy affecting water. Knowing the properties of water, a person can change its structure through music. For example, classical, spiritual, and positive music creates beautiful crystals. And music with the opposite structures makes it ugly. I highly recommend you to read Emoto's book, I think you will find answers to many questions.

Effects of music on plants

In the 20th century, many studies were conducted that showed that music has a powerful effect on plants as well. Many CDs are even sold today to stimulate plant growth. Plant growth primarily depends on the purity of sounds.

For example, tropical plants grow very well under the sounds of modern rap. The effect of music depends on the resonance mechanism, which contributes to the accumulation of energy and the acceleration of metabolism in the plant organism. Resonance is a physical phenomenon that modulates the amplitude of oscillations in a system when the frequency of oscillations from an external source approaches the frequency of natural oscillations in the system.

The phenomenon of resonance depends on synchronization. During synchronization, an oscillation mode is established in which the frequencies are equal or multiples of each other.

The sound signal is perceived by the resonant systems of plants, beetles, and tissues.

Research done for plants

In the 70s, American scientist Dorothy Retallack conducted a study. She used special chambers, strictly approved, with conditions of light, humidity, and temperature.

She placed the 10-day-old plant shots here. There were 3 groups of plants. The first group did not listen to music, the second group listened to music for 3 hours a day, and the third group listened to music for 8 hours a day.

As a result, plants in group 2 grew significantly compared to plants in group 1, while plants in group 3 died after 2 weeks.

It has also become clear that Bach and Indian melodic compositions have a very good effect on plants. But in company with rock music, their leaves shrink. In 1979, Dan Carlson conducted research in the United States that developed a technique to stimulate plant growth. He called it the "sounding flower". In the 70s in Sweden, it was also found that plants grow faster under the influence of music.

Thus it becomes clear to us that music has a great influence on nature. If we think very deeply about this subject, we will understand that the small phenomena of nature are followed by the larger phenomena. First of all, the fact that everything is interconnected in this world, in the universe, and on our planet, we can assume that nature gets the dose of music it needs. It comes even from nature, air, and micro-sounds.

Nature thrives on positive music, thus nurturing the smaller micronutrients. If we understand the scientific and even non-scientific explanation of all this, we will understand the exceptional truth that music is simply a miraculous gift from the universe...

But we will come back to that topic later.

Spiritual music and its influence

Everyone has the right to believe or not believe in God. Therefore, everyone has a choice whether to listen to spiritual music or not... But the fact is that spiritual optimistic compositions have a very good effect on a person mentally and physically. It doesn't have to be specifically religious or church-related, but at least I want to introduce you to the types of spiritual music as I want to explain afterward how it can have a wonderful effect on ailments and moods.

Here are the genres that are also used by the church:

- Organ music
- Music for other musical instruments
- Music for orchestra, soloists, and organ
- Choral
- Solo
- Solo with instrumental accompaniment
- Parade music
- Music to serve God
- Prayer-meditation music

I want to draw your attention to a vaguely meditative style of music because I believe it is beyond Christian, Muslim, or other religious egregores and has a wide platform for improvisation.

Why... Because it does not have a specific name, address, specific God, or saint. But if we want to compose in that genre, we will find a greater platform by focusing on the human subconsciousness using meditations, also from the point of view of prayer, praying at the same time, and believing in the productivity of the given composition, at the same time using necessary musical instruments that we already know have an effect on the brain. I want to mention a very important fact, which I will come back to in more detail shortly.

Why, when during meditation a person talks about the present time, it happens faster, it helps to achieve the result rather than if, for example, while meditating we talk about the result, about feeling good in the future... There is a very important and deep explanation for this...

Meditation as a way to change reality

Currently, many studies are made on how meditation affects our brains, and many experiments are done every week. It provides many neurological benefits, from changes in the gray matter of the brain to activation of certain brain center functions. It helps to reduce nervous states and improves attention and psychological state.

I would like to mention a few facts about meditation.

1. Meditation keeps the aging brain active.

A study conducted at ULLA University showed that long-term meditation rejuvenates our brain: participants who had meditated for up to 20 years had greater gray matter volume in their brains than those who did not meditate.

2. Meditation reduces the activity of the "I" center of the brain.

One of the most interesting experiments in recent years was conducted by Yale University. It proved that meditation reduces the activity of the default mode neuron- DMN, which is responsible for the so-called monkey mind.

The sleep network is switched on or active when we are not thinking about anything or when our mind is jumping from thought to thought. Although mind-wandering is usually associated less with songwriting and more with worry about the past and future, many people aim to alleviate it.

And this study showed that meditation does just that with the DMN. As soon as the mind begins to wander, meditators are better able to stop the collision because of the new connections that are formed.

3. The effects of meditation on depression and anxiety are comparable to those of antidepressants.

A study at John Hopkins University showed that the effect of meditation on pain, anxiety, and depression was 0.3 points. Let me say that the antidepressant effect is another 0.3 points. In fact, apart from this, meditation is also an active exercise for our brain. Many people think that listening to meditation does nothing, but it is actually a magical medicine for the brain.

4. Meditation can lead to changes in key brain volumes.

In 2011, Sarah Lazar and her team at Harvard found that meditation can change the structure of the brain. By meditating consciously for eight weeks, a person increases the thickness of the hippocampal cortex (MRSR), which controls memory and learning, as well as parts of the brain responsible for controlling emotions. In the process of realizing one's own "I".

It also reduces the volume of cells responsible for fear, anxiety, and stress. Our subjective perceptions and feelings change. I think it is very well understood by all of us how important things they found out.

5.Even a few days of exercise improves focus and concentration.

Today, the problem of concentration is not only a problem for children but also for adults. This is one of the best aspects of meditation itself that it improves focus, even after a few sessions. People who meditated before the exam scored 16 percent higher.

To my mind, it will be officially used in scientific institutions soon.

6. Meditation reduces anxiety and social phobia

There is Mindfulness-Based Stress Reduction (MBSR), developed by Jon Kabat Jean at the University of Massachusetts. It's available across the US today. The goal of the method is to reduce stress.

Studies have shown that with this method, there is a result just after 8 weeks of using it. It even has some effects several years later. It helps to get rid of social phobia.

7. Meditation helps to get rid of addiction

Research has shown that meditation helps break addictions by affecting the areas of the brain responsible for self-control. An American program entitled "freedom from smoking" proved that after 17 weeks of work, people quit smoking more easily.

Through meditation, one separates the state of desire from the act of smoking, realizing that they are not necessarily related.

How our brain works

Neurons

Neurons are the basic so-called building blocks of our brains. They are 86 billion. One neuron is activated 5-50 times per second. On average, each neuron has more than five thousand connections with its coefficients. As you read this sentence, billions of neurons are firing signals in your head, neurons in a very complex system that allow us to sense and record every action we've ever had. This is the central basis of teaching. For example, by paying attention or worrying, we create some connections between individual neurons. Neurons are required to transmit signals more often and faster. Therefore, to save energy, the brain creates new structures for specific tasks. This is how we learn new things, using what scientists call neuroplasticity.

Neuroplasticity

Our brain is very flexible, like plasticine. The lifestyle of our life determines its structure and form. This process is very similar to exercise. For example, doing 30 approaches in the gym might not make your muscles stronger, but repeating it for a year will give you results. Similarly, the brain changes shape over time.

Reptilian brain

The human brain can be divided into 3 parts: the reptilian brain, the limbic system, and the cortex.

The reptilian brain is the oldest layer of the brain. In the course of evolution, it appeared first. This part of the brain is responsible for support functions such as body temperature, heart rate, and breathing. This structure governs our instincts, the self-preservation instinct and the survival instinct. For example, when you are anxious and drink alcohol, the reptilian brain feels defeated.

Limbic system

The limbic system combines several structures located above the reptilian brain. The main components are the hippocampus, amygdala, and hypothalamus. The hippocampus is responsible for forming memories. The amygdala is responsible for anxiety or anger. It also determines the strength and brightness of remembered events, due to which they remain in memory for a long time with emotions.

The hypothalamus connects the brain to the endocrine system and helps with the stress response. It sends chemical signals that stimulate or inhibit the production of stress hormones.

The cortex

The cortex is the freshest of all 3 sections. It consists of gray matter that surrounds the deeper white matter of the cerebral hemispheres.

Gray matter contains the bodies of neurons, white matter consists of fibers that connect gray matter cells.

The cortex is responsible for higher-order operations such as abstract thinking and problem-solving ability. This part of the brain makes us different from animals.

The brain's response to stress

During stress, the 3 main structures of the limbic system, the hippocampus, amygdala, and hypothalamus work together.

For example, you are standing in a field and you notice a body that looks like a snake. The hypothalamic memory tells you that you are afraid of a snake, this activates the amygdala, the brain's fear center, which in turn affects the hypothalamus.

The hypothalamus sends a signal to the pineal gland, which sends information to the adrenal glands, which release cortisol. Cortisol is the main stress hormone that tells the body whether to fight or escape.

Neurophysiology of the unconscious state

The cortex, limbic system, and reptilian system work together. They are connected by white matter. For example, in snakes, the salivation instinct is activated by the limbic system, which produces cortisol in the body. This momentary programmed reflex can bring one out of sudden danger.

At the same time, the rational part of the brain, the cortex, evaluates the situation. It's a slower process. The cerebral cortex may not be able to cope with the increased activity of the limbic system or may not be able to logically suppress irrational fears. We don't really know how it works, we only know a certain percentage about our brain.

Take your emotions hostage

Daniel Goleman called it emotional hijacking when our amygdala screams about something.

This happens when something in the environment causes stress. For example, someone raises their voice, criticizes you, or scares you. From the point of view of neurophysiology, the functioning of the visual and auditory systems depends on the activity of the amygdala, which causes a stress response. This is the peak of evolution as a reaction to stress. But stress is caused not only by external stimuli but also by our thoughts.

There are 2 types of anxiety: obsessive thoughts about the past and fantasies about the future. These are the worst triggers. Everything in the environment is changeable, but one's thoughts are continuous.

Neurophysiology of thinking

If you constantly worry, get angry, or lie to yourself, eventually the brain will react to it. And vice versa, if you are optimistic, you will change your reality. By practicing neuroplasticity with regular mindfulness practices, you can stabilize yourself to stimuli, and you can manage your emotions.

How does music interact with energy and singing?

We already know the beneficial effects of music on our brain, internal organs, and nervous system. We also already know enough about the effects of meditation to at least start practicing it. As in the case of some pills, if, for example, taking one or more drugs at the same time, some acute conditions or diseases go away faster, so in this case, if we consider music, meditation by singing, or simply listening to that person's singing, but necessarily on a meditative basis. , then we will have the same effect.

As a musician myself, I can say that this method is much more effective when you perform the composition yourself because, undoubtedly, the words spoken from our lips have a stronger effect on the brain than simply heard, but you can also listen to the meditation performed by someone else and repeat mentally to yourself.

This will certainly have a stronger effect than the pills, maybe, maybe an equivalent effect.

This can be called self-medication. Imagine that you are very lonely in the whole world and no psychologist or doctor can cure you. In this case, if you don't start helping yourself, no one will. Start with self-healing, helping yourself.

And believe in your abilities. Believe that meditation with music will have the same effect on your body as pills.

Some scientists have already done experiments in this field.

It is no coincidence that even with spiritual songs, people have cured many diseases. However, our brain gives a clearer response and decides that the reality is what you pronounce than when you hear it from someone else's lips. That's why I want to emphasize that this technique will be more effective if you sing meditative compositions that are designed to fight against health, psychological and mental problems.

You can go a long way with music therapy. Scientists are still half-way, if not at the beginning, to discovering what a piece of magically powerful force music is and how much good it still has to do on our planet. The purpose of that book is optimistic and continuous...Because next, I have to record an album of meditative, upbeat, healing, and mood-changing compositions with clear instrumental accompaniment.

So far, I have written three travel books about beautiful places in the USA, Canada, and Europe. Of course, traveling and self-knowledge are very important for improving the quality of our life, but I want to say that I am first of all a singer, and then I am a writer.

Being in music and singing almost all my life, I have a question and problem about how music can heal us. That is why I want each of you to discover this mysterious miracle in your way, which was given to us from the universe.

No person in the world does not like music. It means it's part of us, we're born and die with music, the music stays...

It is forever and always will be. And so will always be art, love, and darkness. All these will change their form and methods over time because when everything changes and becomes unrecognizable, art will also change, and music will change in its way of expression and perception, but love and faith will always remain in the world. Love is the base of everything... it wasn't just given to us from the universe to just dance to in clubs or listen to - to have a good time. Music has a very important mission on this planet.. if its mysterious nature has not yet been fully revealed, it is equal to the same undiscovered arts, as I mentioned, like love and faith. Because no matter how times change, people will always have it in their lives, regardless of their will, regardless of good or bad events in the world... regardless of wars, happy and sad moments... of all the transitory good and bad values, will go and be forgotten, but the most important of the permanent ones, love, will lead us to the other important value- to music.

And I would love for all of us to try to be closer to our essence, to nature. Music is in our very nature... use it as medicine, as a good friend, as someone who listens to you, supports you in bad situations, and finally as the best doctor.

Epilogue

Among the most important moments in life to be thankful for are the moments when you realize that without important events and people, you wouldn't have what you have and you wouldn't feel what you feel… Would not have had the resources that provided the insight that helped write this book...

I am very grateful for the events that brought me to New York...

I am very grateful to my beloved person who has been by my side all this time and always supports me on all issues... Without great love, there would be no motivation to create something useful for other people...

I am very grateful for life in all its good and bad parts, which has made me this Marianna Lima, who has many things to do in the world, and a desire to be useful to everyone....

I also thank you for reading this far because, without you, this book wouldn't exist...

See you…

Marianna Lima

Marianna Lima is a jazz, soul, gospel, and pop singer. She is the author of three books: "Europe in my heart", "American dream", "Canada".

Marianna Lima has more than twenty international awards from Europe and United States of America. She also arranges her own songs.

This book was written in advance of the project, the purpose of which is to tell people in detail how important the role of music is in our lives, our brain health, goals, well-being, positive thinking, organizing life plans, and everything in general that surrounds us. , which accompanies us from the moment we wake up to the moment we sleep, from the second we are born to the moment we die.

Music is a magical, mysterious power, energy that we receive from the universe as a gift and it is very important to appreciate its meaning and influence in our life.

I hope that as soon as you read it, your attitude and ideas about music, life, and yourself will change. If you use the power of music in your life, you will realize that it is as powerful as a pill, in some cases even more powerful... My goal is to pass on to you the information I have, which I am going to apply with the help of actions and techniques in my project, which has a large-scale goal of bene-fiting humanity.